CW00802047

ACKNOWL]

I would like to thank:

Lydia Dixon for her design for the cover, which accompanies
   𝔜𝔯 𝔚𝔶𝔡𝔡𝔣𝔞 - 𝔗𝔲𝔪𝔲𝔩𝔲𝔰,
Philip Tansen O'Donohoe for helping me find my voice,
our many hosts along the way
my fellow pilgrims for their companionship on the pilgrimage,
and my beloved wife Anne for being there for me.

....

Information about the Pilgrims' Way North Wales
Taith Pererin Gogledd Cymru
can be found at
http://www.pilgrims-way-north-wales.org.

....

Other titles by Aziz Dixon, available or forthcoming on
amazon.co.uk include:
- Sufi Sunrise
- Poem Seeds
- River and Hills: voices of Irwell.

CONTENTS

North Wales Pilgrim: a poetic journey

reflections on a pilgrimage from Holywell to Bardsey, June 2015

May the road rise with you
may the wind be always at your back,
may the sun shine warm upon your face….

....

1. Llanarmon-yn-Ial
Preparation, April 2015

What languages did he speak,
this man of God?
Credo in unum Deum,
Credaf yr Nuw Tad…
i'th glodfori di.

What languages of the heart?
The Gospel of love,
a warrior saint, defeating the 'heathen'
not ten miles from here (it is said);
'Alleluia,' he cried, and they all
turned and fled.

And what of the mujahida,
the greater battle, with the Self?

What did they call him?
Garmon Sant, Germanus,
healer, teacher, brother and friend?

What names did he have for this place,
mam ddeaer, coed, bryn, y gwynt?
What were they to him,
these woods, these hills, mother earth, the wind

and the bright daffodils?

How did he get here from France?
Our pilgrimage has maps, the best of kit,
maybe a phone that is smart;
a map of the heart,
'away from it all' for fifteen days
making
       space
for the inner voice
which is with us always.

Now we shelter in his church, as
children come by, with Resurrection buns.
The deafening - buffeting - wind but a whisper now
as we contemplate
our pilgrimage in an unfamiliar land.

What whispers did he leave
over fifteen hundred years?
A place of worship still here,
a story handed down,
a sense of the sacred in these stones,
this yew tree.

What whispers will I leave
on this land as we walk
in the glance of meeting,
the words of greeting on the journey,
in the hearts of those I love
at the end of my days?

2. What's in a name?
day 1, Maen Achwyfan

Maen Achwyfan – the name of this place:
a monument,
a farm or two, a meeting of lanes.
St Cwyfan's stone, but in what sense his?

Tallest wheelcross in Britain,
Northumbrian tradition with Viking influence,
late tenth century, figure with spear
trampling a serpent, not to mention *the*
interlace designs...

but the technical words fail to convey
the spirit of the place, the smell
of the grass, the signature tune
of these designs, calling, recalling others,
a typology of devotion,
a labour of love to carve it.

So was this the echo of the saint,
and why this spot, like those
we will see at Trelawnyd,
at Tremeirchion too?
Was this where he spoke to them,
a church in the field, not
fixed in glass and stone?

What overlay of meaning do we look for here,
eager to know, to be sure?
Do we otherwise know who he was?
Who was it carved it and why?
Or is it enough to suggest
that over four hundred years
St Cwyfan
inspired this stone?

3. Trelawnyd: early morning
day 2

Hard is the floor of the hall,
hard on my bones and my back.

Will it rain all day today?
Will my boots be still wet?
And will there be a lightness
in my step, as we stride out
once more along the Way?

The liturgy for today:
a crowd of Celtic saints, walking with us,
- and many have healing wells
to show us
from fifteen hundred years ago;
each saint a story, a memory
glimpsed in the village name;
a yew tree older than them all,
a hillfort older still.

The whole Welsh topography
held in the names I only half discern –
walking half blind if with no key
to this most descriptive of tongues:
oak tree pass, place of the big holly tree,
the cold port, the orchard close.
How will it be,
our next hafodunos,
pilgrims' shelter for the night?

Soon I must uncurl, refuel, re-pack.
What do I care
if it rains all day today?

—

8

4. All in a day's walk
day 2, Trelawnyd to St Asaph

Forty-six stiles we have climbed today,
most with an arrow pointing the way,
but each had a character all of its own:
some hugging the nettle and thorn,
or smugly stuck in the slurry,
wood-wet and slip-tippy, rickety,
some made of stone.

The further we go, the higher they get,
forty-six stiles just made for rucksack yoga,
as we balance the weight
we need not have brought.

Now as the rain and the wind
tease, squeal at the window,
I indulge my feet in warm water
and look back on the day.

The stile by the river, sand martins
rejoicing in silent ballet;
the opening to the bluebell wood,
sun-dappled, scent of pine and nettle,
sheep and grass; the fox-holes,
the pheasant running ahead.
The large herd of bullocks
blocking our way; the stile
by the drover's pool, now overrun
by lorries diverted down lanes.
And here, where the railway runs no more;
the ford and the hilltop, a sweeping view
of rain from Denbigh to Rhyl.

Stiles with attitude, all the way,
but of kissing gates – only five,
and they were special.

5. Rhythm of walking
day 3, Afon Aled, approaching Llansannan

Rhythm of walking,
foot-rise, foot-fall;
hour by hour
the landscape changes –
gorse and cows
and waist-high grass.
A meadow in spring
seen at eye level
as we rest in the buttercups,
vetch and clover.

Foot-rise, foot-fall,
mile by mile, the distant coast,
the farm in the valley hollow,
rhythm of walking,
hour by hour.

Rhythm of breathing,
out-breath, in-breath;
la illaha IL Allah,
no reality, only Unity,
there to remember,
breath by breath.
Allahu akhbar,
as Samuel Lewis taught us,
in peace is power.

Breath by breath
the landscape changes.
The rain feeds the holy wells;
the wind, gust-swishing,
snarling, sighing,
rain-sweeping, plays
catch and snatch with my breath –
where does it take it?
Rhythm of walking,
day by day.

Rhythm of living,
step by step,
breath by breath,
year by year.
The landscape, inner and outer
continues to change
beyond recognition.
A pilgrim's gratitude –
rhythm of walking,
moment to moment.

6. Yr Wyddfa – Tumulus

day 4, above Afon Aled,
between Llansannan and Gwytherin

Eternal the mountains that nourished me,
Yr Wyddfa, Tryfan, the Carneddau,
and all of them you can see from here,
for high on the moor they buried me,
with a mound to mark my place.

Now the skylark sings for me,
the curlew calls my name,
and the bright-eyed hare
is nestling there,
in the place where
they buried
me.

7. Industrial Revelation
day 6, Great Orme, Llandudno (rest day)

I come from a land of dark decaying mills,
where the cotton, the rain and the hills
define the landscape still.
The industrial sprawl is softer now,
but the riches are there to see –
the old town hall (which they want to pull down)
and the fine Carnegie library.

But here on the Orme,
with the chough, the 'common' rock rose
and the butterfly, which lives
nowhere else in the world,
here they dug for the gold that is green.

Before St Tudno came, when
Stonehenge was not yet a project plan,
with stones from the beach and animal bones,
they dug and they delved
for the malachite ore
to smelt the Bronze
that defines their Age
(so we say.)

Child labour and slag-heaps
and riches for some –
the pace of change is faster now
after four thousand years,
but have we all changed
so very much?

8. Hiraeth
day 7, Rowen

'Have ever you seen the like of this?'
the care-taker said to me.
'I love this chapel, I love these hills,
this green, always-green,
the saints and the spirits of home.
Hiraeth we call it,'
the pull of the place where I belong.

I know this well, as we pass Peel Tower,
or crest the top of the Grane,
and there in the Valley is Rawtenstall,
a ribbon-flower enfolded by moors,
a garden of peace and plenty.

Hiraeth – is it Ishkh as well,
the longing of Love,
Lover and Beloved in One,
the place inside
where I belong?

9. Walking for Jesus
day 7, Rowen to Llanfairfechan

Above Conwy castle we stop for lunch,
looking back at the way we have come.
We all like the sheep, as they scatter
past us, bleating in disarray.

Last night we missed the male voice choir,
but maybe Handel came this way.
In St Celynin's church, remotest of all,
with St Celynin's newts in St Celynin's holy well,
we met the Jesus Army, looking for signs.
They sang, and they blessed, and they
filled the chapel with joy.
'Take this cross,' one of them said,
'Carry it on to Bardsey.'

All we like sheep
have gone astray,
(the tenors most of all)
we have turn-ed
every one to his own way,

and the Lord hath laid,
hath laid on Him
the InIquity
of us
        all.

10. Mara
day 8, Abergwyngregin to Llanllechid

A girl, her Dad and her teddy
came walking this way today.
He stopped for her, and as they talked
he shared his love of the hills.

About that age, a lad and his Dad,
at the bluebell time of the year
went walking in Wales –
explorers together – and the dad,
he shared his love of the hills.

About this age, a Dad and his girls –
on an Orkney picnic at Birsay:
a tidal road, we test the ebb,
hand in hand we cross the sea.
Childhood rests on the farther shore,
a place no more to be reached,

for a parent's love is a delicate thing
to nurture and yet let go.

11. Lines of Power
day 8, Abergwyngregin to Llanllechid

Telford's road, Edward's castle,
even Stephenson's tubular bridge
at Conwy, all seem
to fit the lie of the land,
but whose are these lines of power
imposed eighty years ago?

Ignoring the contours, they march
straight
over Penmaenmawr,
the way the Romans came,
above the Bronze Age stones;
leaping this valley, the river with three names,
above the kite with angle-poise wings.

The light and the heat we need indeed,
but if today we had the power,
would we not wish to channel it
under the ground?

12. The magic of the moor
day 9, Bangor to Llanberis

'Come this way,' the cuckoo calls,
but the path is undefined,
the ground is wet, and a kestrel
drops like a stone.
The clouds are dark and low,
the whinberries hard and green,
and a mist of fatigue
descends on the moor,
sweeps suddenly over us all.

Is that a magic bridge I see,
spanning the valley from ridge to ridge?
Will the wild horses carry my pack?
Are there sherpas just waiting for me
in the derelict farm beneath the trees?
Or is it all a mirage of the moor?

We plod to the top, and over the col
for lunch,
and there on the mountain straight ahead
white puffs of smoke, a mirage on the hill;

but this time it's real – for Snowdon is there,
and just beyond those mines,
a train really is climbing
the 'Pile of Stones.'

13. Wachet auf!
day 10, Llanberis

Sleepers wake, the blackbird calls us!

In the first light of dawn,
the air thick with sleep,
and the promise of another day,
walking with the faith of a Bach chorale
in this non-Conformist land,

the blackbird sings outside my window,
each note calling me
up steps of stillness to the light.

I turn, and he wakes you too,
and I gaze with gratitude
on your beautiful face.

14. Passage of time
day 11, Waun Fawr to Penygroes

We met St Garmon again today –
our water was straight from his well.
The mountains were stunning, but ever so hot,
and I rested my face in wild thyme
when we stopped near St Tyrog's grave.

Heron guards the deep quarry
where Darwin might have stood,
when the rocks spoke to him
of the passage of glacial time.

Hot, hotter still, and weary now;
the valley of slate has homes and hearths
roofless and doorless, plaques
torn from the graves,
reclaimed by the birds and the sheep,
all ghosted with passage of time.

And down in the valley, it's nearly all shut;
the trains are long gone, and the couple we meet
tell us again of the passage of time.
'I was born in that house,
sixty shops there were then,
sixty years since we were wed.'

Now late at night in the shimmering heat,
counting sheep with my pulse,
a call from the past, unheard for years,
a nightjar answers the owl.

May I be serene, Mrs Gentle, and loving,
as we walk hand in hand,
with the passage of time.

15. Unflinching
day 12, Clynnog Fawr to Morfa Nefyn

This could be St Beuno's day,
his shrine at Clynnog a rallying point
for pilgrims, a spacious surprise,
elegant, light. His well
we clean, and later we find
his herb-strewn chapel,
with Celtic font, resting
by the sea.

Proper pilgrims we, we spurn the bus
that would have stopped for us. But soon,
the heat and the blisters tell on us,
skin raw and sore in the shimmering sun.

Edgar Christian starved to death –
he came from a village near here.
Exploring the Arctic was his pilgrimage,
his diary 'Unflinching,' his courage undimmed.

Too many miles we have walked again,
and to think that on starting
I feared the rain!
Still, St Beuno's here, and
there's no discouragement
would make me once relent
my first avowed intent
to be a pilgrim.

16. St Beuno's, Pistyll
day 12

Older than all of this quiet sanctuary,
the font that St Beuno might have seen
in a dream.

Life is like a Celtic design –
so much detail seen close up,
a pattern of beauty seen from above,
a rhythm of pattern becoming
memories over time.

The artist's skill
leaps the years; life's knots
and life's threads of untying
still to be traced,
set in stone for those pilgrims
who follow us.

17. Listening out for history
day 12, Nefyn

People talk to us as we walk,
tell us things that could otherwise go missing
in this fly-in -- > drive-by -- > WhatsApp world.
Brother Francis and his friars' scarf, and
a sprawling disused quarry, maybe
the source for Liverpool's docks.

And here in Nefyn, where a rescuer brings us
tea in the old chandler's shop, in
Y Maes - this narrow street,
between chip-shop and pub?
Well, it *led to* a wide open space,
where Edward came to celebrate,
held his tournament (the Englishman said.)

What else goes missing, when unasked?
How to read beyond the word-of-mouth?
Listening at walking-speed,
taking an earful of the landscape,
the landscape whispers back – we are
knee-deep in history.

18. The colour of sleep
day 13, Morfa Nefyn to Llangwnnadl

If God were inclined to go painting,
I'm sure we would know S/he is here.
For the landscape is different,
but the beauty, the colours amazing.
There is primrose yellow, buttercup yellow,
the gorse and the vetch;
grass green, nettle green, kelp green;
purple of orchid and foxglove,
wild mint that is purple and green;
plummeting tern-white, gannet-white,
chough-black, raven-black
and the kittiwakes sail here too.

The sea and the sky embrace,
misty blue lost in wonder at
misty shades of grey;
the thrift a profusion of shades,
pink cascades down the cliffs
to the shore, where time laps
listlessly.

Petrog the seal, the rock that barks,
and his camouflaged kin
(the ones that carry no packs)
watch our painful progress
with mild surprise.

We call the good shepherd, who
rescues one of his flock,
too weak and too sick to care.
Towards evening Gopala arrives:
we explain to the bullocks, who
would otherwise herd us
over the edge.

The sea and the sky part company,
dark deeps touching feathery whisps

of cloud. Down in the cove
it's bedtime for ducklings,
a family all at sea, shellduck parents
shielding their offspring,
keeping the largest of gulls at bay.

Time laps at our heels;
it's time to stop painting,
to find our bed for the night, and explore
the colour of sleep.

19. Arrrival
day 14, Llangwnnadl to Aberdaron

Today begins like any other day.
Hineni, here I am, Lord,
use me for the purpose
that Thy wisdom chooseth.

Like any other day,
we lose our way in the field
(exit top left or top right?),
we cajole the inquisitive bullocks
into letting us pass.

But today is also this moment, this time, this place.
For us the hafodunos at Llangwnnadl
is a caravan; St Gwynhoedl's cae eisteddfa,
pilgrims' place of sitting, his church
and his holy well wait
for another time.

Light rain settles the dust. The sea,
the seal's way, the whale-road,
the gull's space calls to the Seafarer
(though the crossing to Bardsey
is tomorrow, inshAllah.)

Yet today is different too,
for today we arrive. This time
the kissing gate gives onto
suburbs, for all of a hundred yards,
the buildings flowing down to the stream
at our destination, the church on the beach.

In St Hywyn's the local poet, word-woven tranquility
speaks from wall to wall,
a meeting of head and heart,
desert wisdom in this watery place.
Offered thoughts – this pilgrimage as life's journey,

this convergence of coasts where the boat-man
Colin awaits, to ferry us across to the after-life.
This a Christian metaphor too,
read in Senacus's stone by the altar. The church
is filled with immanent light. Light
breathes me.

To arrive is to open, within,
to begin again, and to renew
like a Celtic spiral,
sustained by the caravan of saints
who have walked ahead,
all the illuminated souls
who form the embodiment of the Master,
the spirit of guidance.

To arrive within, bismillah,
toward the One,
a depth unlooked for, sharing
with you eternity's light caresses,
each breath, each step
the way of a pilgrim.
Ya Shakur – the joy of gratitude.

20. Waste not, want not: urban myth
Llandudno

I am an eco-warrior,
one of the town vigilantes.
All our gang have fine pink feet.
Our mission is to stop the waste –
so much food would be lost
without us, but they do not understand,
these crazy bipeds.

I have my own patch to patrol –
not the seafront for me.
There's a bus shelter right outside
the upmarket chip shop, and often
I can catch their eye,
when they're enjoying a meal.
Anything not eaten, and
I'll yodel all across town
(I'm rather proud of my yodelling,
actually.)
Then
we'll swoop in the street
on the unsuspecting, the gull-ible,
seizing chips, sampling
the cod in batter (on a good day) -
just to teach them a lesson.
First done, help the others,
as my Grandad used to say.

21. Waste not, want not: rural idyll
Aberdaron

I, to be frank, am a country sort –
Llandudno's too busy for me.
I have my own place in Aberdaron.
My favourite food is fresh from the stream,
or sometimes the shore – but I do like
to be tidy. Indeed, I'll defend my pitch
if I need to, on the tin roof
of siop Spar.
Every day
at closing time I drop in,
folding my wings elegantly. I'm sure
I blend in with the grey of the roof.
I can be patient, and
my timing's impeccable.
And every day they have food,
just for me to tidy up.
It's a good life, being a heron, but
I'm glad I'm not a vigilante.

22. Time to sit
day 15, Ynys Enlli

Pilgrims from all over Britain
are making for Bardsey today.
The twitter has tweeted,
it's the biggest of twitches
in the bird-warden's whole career.
On this island of saints,
home to Essylt, Iarddur, Bardr the Viking,
poet Meilyr Brydydd and thousands of souls departed,
a mindful procession of walkers,
faces intense with religious zeal,
steps slowly through the fields,
seeking, radioing each revelation.

God has blessed this numinous island
with puffins and peregrines,
shearwaters only at night,
'Welsh penguins' and seals –
St Cuthbert would skip for joy –
but the birders migrating from Devon
have only one thing on their minds:
to find Cretzschmar, telephoto
his bunting, and catch the boat
home for their tea.

The party of seals, on a Sunday outing
(though with no chapel tea)
basking, swimming, chatting,
here they live day to day, but we,
we have met with the weaver,
her willows remind us of home.

We have walked to the end.
Now we have time,

just to sit
in the silence in the mind,
in the bright field,
hand in hand,
just to be
.

....

...may the sun shine warm upon your face,
may the rain fall soft upon your fields
and until we meet again
may God hold you
in the hollow of Her hand.

Made in the USA
Charleston, SC
25 September 2015